Mona Lisa
and the others

Alice Harman

Illustrated by
Quentin Blake

Contents

LEONARDO DA VINCI (1452–1519)

Mona Lisa

1503–1519   Oil paint on wood

Leonardo da Vinci was an Italian painter, engineer, draftsman, sculptor, architect, and scientist. He lived and worked during the Renaissance period.

Welcome to the book!

Hello! I . . . um . . . ugh, sorry, I always get so awkward about introducing myself! It feels kind of fake to act like I don't know I'm probably the **most famous painting in the world**, but I don't want people to think I'm snooty about it.

Boo hoo, poor me, right? Having millions of people coming to see me every year, and my face on everything from T-shirts to teapots. Such a tough life. Don't get me wrong, it's **lovely** that people are excited to see me, but I sometimes feel like I'm hogging all the attention without meaning to!

The truth is, as proud as I am to have been painted by an artist **as brilliant as Leonardo**, there are so many other artists and artworks that deserve to be seen and admired, too.

It makes me feel kind of bad—and it annoys more than a few of my neighbors here at the Louvre Museum in Paris . . .

So I've made sure that this book is full of all sorts of amazing works of art, all found here at the Louvre, and that they get a chance to **tell their own stories**. And I'll be taking this chance to tell mine, too.

You might like some artworks more than others—you might like some more than you like me! **And that's absolutely fine.** Art is a million times more fun when you forget the dusty old SHOULDs and MUSTs, and just enjoy it—whatever way you want! And if anyone asks "Where did you hear that nonsense?" you can tell them: "Mona Lisa said so."

STOP! THIEF!

Did you know that I was once stolen, **right off the walls of the Louvre**? Seriously! I went missing for two years. It started one dark night in 1911. I was minding my own business, having a little snooze, when someone snatched me. I ended up hidden away in Italy, kept by a man who looked strangely familiar . . . Eventually, this man got in touch with an art dealer to sell me. As if there hadn't been a worldwide hunt for me for the last two years!

Long story short, the police got the man and I made it safely back to the Louvre. And it suddenly hit me: I *did* know the man who took me—he had worked at the Louvre! He was Italian and said he stole me because I belonged back in Italy, where Leonardo and

I were "born." But do you know who the police suspected at first? Pablo Picasso! Yes, the artist! He and a famous poet, Guillaume Apollinaire, were both arrested. They were part of an out-there, super-modern group of creatives known as "The Wild Men of Paris." Some people thought they stole me to blow a big raspberry at the old world of art that I stood for.

Anyway, when I arrived back at the Louvre it was clear that my quiet, respectable fame had **skyrocketed**! Some people still like to keep the mystery alive today, claiming that I'm a fake and the original *Mona Lisa* was never returned. Experts agree that I'm the real thing, but I don't worry about proving myself. **I just smile on,** like I've got a secret I'll never tell . . .

where on Earth am I?

You might have heard people talking about the mystery of my not-quite-there smile, but **you know what's really mysterious**? Take a look behind me. The lonely winding road, the jagged mountains, the forbidding waters and gloomy sky . . . I mean, where am I supposed to be?!

Some people think it's an actual place in Italy, which has a bridge like the one just above my left shoulder. But, **real or not**, Leonardo chose to paint the landscape in an otherworldly way.

Meanwhile, I'm sitting on a normal chair, wearing normal (for the time) clothes.

Celebs have feelings, too!

Sometimes I worry that people have **such big expectations** of me that I can't possibly measure up. Literally: visitors always go on about how tiny I am!

My colors aren't bright and flashy, either. But see how my hair, my sleeves, my eyes, and the landscape behind my shoulders all have a warm, coppery tone? It hurts my feelings when people call my colors "dull," but **not because I'm vain—promise!** It just feels like they're not looking closely enough. Leonardo meant for me to have this hazy, dreamy look. He used a painting technique called *sfumato* to make my colors fade into each other in a soft, smoky way. Try to spot harsh lines or brushstrokes: I don't think you'll be able to find any!

9

LEONARDO DA VINCI

Portrait of an Unknown Woman

around 1490–1497   Oil paint on wood

Leonardo da Vinci was an Italian painter, engineer, draftsman, sculptor, architect, and scientist. He lived and worked during the Renaissance period.

why her?

WHAT is the big deal about Mona Lisa? Can anyone tell me? We're both painted by Leonardo, we're both mysterious, and yet nobody knows anything about me. Where are my crowds of fans? My worldwide fame? My own special waiting-line system because everyone wants to lay eyes on me?

I mean, sure, people APPRECIATE me, but it's not the same. It's not Mona Lisa-mania! Is there something really special about her— or **is it all just luck** and timing?

Mona Lisa definitely got a fame boost from being stolen (see page 8), but she was outshining me well before that! In our time, tons of artists wanted to copy the way Leonardo painted her. And did you know that Napoleon I hung her painting in his bedroom for a while before taking her to the Louvre?

But I do wonder, **is she now just famous for being famous**?! Do me a favor: flick back and forth between page 6 and page 10. Do you think there's something extra special about Mona Lisa? If so, **can you describe what it is?** I can take it, promise!

Venus de Milo

150–125 BCE Marble
Greek island of Melos (now Milos)

Many works of art from the ancient world were created by artists whose names have not been recorded. Venus de Milo was discovered in an ancient Greek ruin.

One thing I know for sure is there's **no such thing** as "most beautiful woman." Ideas about beauty change over time and in different parts of the world. That's a fact. So instead of just judging what is and isn't beautiful, it's **waaaay more interesting** to think about how and why we picture "beautiful" the way we do.

I mean, people think I'm so elegant in my cool white marble, but back in 150 BCE I'm pretty sure I was painted in **super-bright colors**— and I've still got little holes from where I wore actual metal jewelry! Can you imagine that?

Do you know what's really beautiful? The **love and care** that the artist who made me put into their work. My marble isn't smooth and flat: it bulges and ripples and folds like a human body.

My favorite parts are the little ones most people don't notice. The flare of my nostrils, the creases across my neck, the flesh where my chest meets my arm, the inside of my belly button. Can you find any other details like these, that look too real to be made of rock?

It's not a beauty contest!

Everyone thinks we're not going to get along, me and Mona—like we're in some mean-girl competition. "**YOU'RE the beautiful one!**" people always tell me. "The most beautiful woman in the world!" And I'm like, *so*?

Look, I love looking at beautiful art. But I'm **so much more** than just the beauty with the broken-off arms. I've been on this Earth for over 2,000 years—I know some stuff!

One of the reasons it's hard to know for sure if I'm actually Aphrodite/Venus or not is because of my **missing arms**. See, ancient Greek art often tells you who the different gods and goddesses are by showing them holding their particular "attribute"—usually a special object or animal.

Now, obviously, without my arms attached no one can see the clues that would probably have been in my hands. I'm a mystery woman; I could be anyone! So why do experts think I'm Aphrodite? Well, apparently, um, my **lack of clothes** is a big clue. And people say that a hand holding an apple, which is an Aphrodite attribute, was found near to where I was dug up.

But there are people who think I might not be Aphrodite at all. They imagine from my **twisted pose** what my arms might be doing: holding a spear, spinning thread, looking in a handheld mirror. What do you think I could be up to?

Actually Aphrodite?

The world knows me as the Venus de Milo, but I'd like to take this opportunity to reintroduce myself. Hi, nice to meet you, **I'm Aphrodite**! Well, um, probably. OK, let me explain. Venus was the ancient Roman name for Aphrodite, who was the ancient Greek **goddess of love.** I was made in ancient Greek times and found in ancient Greece, so I'm more an Aphrodite than a Venus. Buuut, it's not quite that simple. I was found on the island of Melos, or Milo, hence my name. And lots of people there worshipped a sea goddess called **Amphitrite**, who looked distinctly Aphrodite-ish. I wish I could remember, but it was so long ago . . .

From rubble to riches

So, for the last 200-odd years I've been hanging out in the Louvre. But do you know where I lived before that? **In a hole in the ground!**

Yeah, seriously. And I might have stayed there forever if a man called Yorgos hadn't needed to build a wall. He dug up the stones above my head . . . but they weren't just any old stones. They were part of an **ancient Greek ruin**.

Well, long story short, I caught the eye of the Marquis de Rivière, the French ambassador to the Ottoman Empire, and after a bumpy boat journey I made it **all the way to France**. Then I was given as a present to King Louis XVIII!

The King decided to donate me to the Louvre so that **everyone** could see me. And, look, I know that sounds like how a king might politely get rid of an unwanted gift, but **he really did like me**! He used to come and look at me in the Louvre (even though he was very old and ill by then). How's that for moving up in the world?

REMBRANDT VAN RIJN (1606–1669)

self-Portrait at the Easel

1660 Oil paint on canvas

Rembrandt van Rijn—known by his first name, Rembrandt—was a Dutch painter, printmaker, and draftsman. He worked during the 17th century, which is known as the Dutch Golden Age of painting.

Not a pretty picture?

Ah, hello there. You'll forgive me if I don't stay to talk long. I have a painting to finish. See the long brush in one hand, the pot of tools in the other, and the artist's easel in front of me? Oh, who am I kidding? You must forgive an old(ish) man his vanity. The truth is that **it's ME**, not my talents, under the spotlight here.

My critics said that I "loved **ugliness** more than beauty." But I always thought it was a shame they had such a narrow idea of beauty. I could have made myself youthful and stunningly handsome, but I chose to paint in all my lines and shadows and soft, sagging skin. Because that was my face, and I could see my **whole life** within it.

Light and shadow

Did you notice how my face is lit up? How **brightness** bounces off one side and makes my (now very out of style) white hat positively glow? I'm quite proud of that. In fact, I'm famous for creating light in my paintings that looks **almost magical**, like it's shining from within.

Do you want to know my secret? Shadow. To appreciate the full beauty of the light, you need to show it coming out of the **darkness**. It's a painting technique called *chiaroscuro*, but for me it runs deeper. The truth is that in life there is no light without dark, no joy without sadness, no bravery without fear. And I want to **show it all**.

The truth isn't always pretty, but it has a beauty all of its own. That's what I tried to show in my paintings.

Winged Human-Headed Bulls

717–706 BCE   Marble

These bulls with human heads originate from modern-day Iraq and date from the 8th century BCE. They once stood at the entrance to the palace of the Assyrian king Sargon II in Khorsabad.

Big friendly giants

"Hello there!"

"Hello from me, too! I'm on the right, see?"

"We're kind of a . . ."

*". . . **double act!**"*

"I know we look kind of intimidating. More than twice the size of a tall adult human, with big stomping bull hooves, gigantic eagle wings, a stony gaze, and not a single curly hair out of place. But **we're nice**, promise! We're even smiling, see?"

*"Yeah, we're lamassu. Or lumasi, or aladlammû— so good they named us three times, I always say! Around 2,700 years ago, King Sargon II ordered sixty or so of us to be built, to protect his new palace and capital city from enemies of his Assyrian Empire—and to support the doorways. **Magical AND practical**, go us!"*

"But when Sargon died, the new Assyrian king wanted his own shiny new city. So our city, Dur Sharrukin, was abandoned and the desert sand swallowed us up."

*"Ugh, I'm STILL finding grains of that sand in my mouth. Anyway, we were dug out about 200 years ago and brought here. Still together, and **still best friends**, after all these years."*

How many legs?

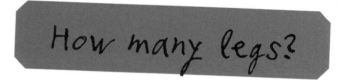

"Hey, how many legs do we have?"

*"**Four**, right? Bulls have four legs. Hmmm, let me check. Oh wow, there are **five** of them!"*

"Cool, right? So from the front it looks like we're standing to attention, and from the side it looks like we're walking."

*"Best of both worlds! Weren't our makers also obsessed with using **really precise math** to get us looking perfect?"*

"Yeah, that's right. All that fussing was kind of annoying at the time, but we do look sharp!"

GEORGES DE LA TOUR (1593?–1652)

The Cheat With the Ace of Diamonds

around 1632–1640   Oil paint on canvas

Georges de La Tour was a French painter who worked in the mid-17th century.
He is known for his atmospheric candlelit scenes.

who are you calling a cheat?!

The absolute nerve of it, I tell you! Little Miss Mona Lisa **pulls a mysterious expression**, and people fly across the world to swoon at her. But I do the same and I'm labeled a cheat!

Of course, the problem is that I'm centerstage—which is understandable, given my **fabulous outfit**—so people think that the "cheat" in the painting's title is me. But look what my dashing friend on the left is holding behind his back . . . yes, that card is the Ace of Diamonds. **HE's the cheat!** Can you see how La Tour even painted him in shadow? He was making it perfectly clear who the shady one was, if only people paid attention.

Apparently people think I'm in on the scam, along with the servant, because of our "shifty" looks. Rude! But frankly, that silly boy on the right deserved to be cheated anyway. Flashing his gold coins around, **trying to outshine me** with his over-decorated clothes . . . maybe someone needed to teach him a lesson.

Comeback (de La) Tour

I know it's hard to believe that a painting starring myself would **ever fall out of fashion**—but, alas, that was the case for many years. La Tour was forgotten about after his death in 1652 and his work was only rediscovered more than 250 years later. What a long, lonely wait that was . . .

But once "my" painting (oops, La Tour hates when I call it that) had sparked the art world's interest, people went **wild** for his other masterpieces too, and we all made our way back into the spotlight. Don't you just love a happy ending?

Scepter of Charles V
("The Charlemagne Scepter")

around 1364–1380

Gold with pearls, rubies, and colored glass

It is thought that this scepter was made by
Hennequin du Vivier, a goldsmith who worked
in the late Middle Ages, for the French king
Charles V, who ruled from 1364 to 1380.
Later, at the time of the emperor Napoleon,
a goldsmith called Biennais made
a new shaft for the scepter.

Gaze upon my greatness!

Look at me! Look how **GOLD** I am. As IF I needed any introduction, I am the **great and glorious** Emperor Charlemagne. Back in my day, around 1,200 years ago, I ruled over most of Europe. And 550 years later, I was still so adored that King Charles V put me on this scepter to link us together and convince people that he was **the rightful king of France**.

I was made by the King's **goldsmith** (someone who makes objects out of gold). And he did a wonderful job, I must say. Solid gold studded with pearls and rubies? Check. Finely engraved panels celebrating my legendary life? Check. Me sitting **majestically** on a throne, with a crown on my head and eagles under my armpits? Check! LOVE my armpit eagles.

The kingmaker

Do you see the long, fancy-topped stick I'm holding? That's a scepter. So I'm **part of a scepter, holding a scepter**. But what is a scepter FOR, you ask? Well, you usually just sort of hold it and **look kingly**, or queenly, or—in my case—emperorly. (And maybe verrry discreetly scratch hard-to-reach itches . . .)

But I'm a very SPECIAL scepter. I'm part of the French Crown Jewels. Since I was made, I've been used in the **crowning ceremony** for almost every king of France. See the flower my throne is resting on? That six-petaled lily is a symbol of the French kingdom. No more kings in France now, though—the French Revolution was QUITE clear about that! So now I'm sitting back and enjoying my retirement.

VERONESE (PAOLO CALIARI) (1528–1588)

The Wedding Feast at Cana

1562–1563   Oil paint on canvas

Paolo Caliari—known as Veronese, because he came from Verona—was an Italian painter who worked during the Renaissance period. He is known for big, colorful, detailed paintings.

"Hellooo! Over here, on the left! I'm in red and blue, and my lovely wife is next to me in pale blue."

"You were probably expecting us to be **centerstage***, given that we're the bride and groom, and this is our wedding feast and all."*

"But no, that's Jesus, forever known as the star of OUR wedding. Just look at the glowing spotlight that Veronese has given him."

"Unbelievable. He's literally **stolen our spotlight***!"*

"Everyone else in this book is moaning about Mona Lisa getting all the attention around here, but at least they're the **stars** of their own artworks! Must be nice . . ."

"You know the worst part? People expect us to be GRATEFUL to Jesus! For performing his first ever miracle at our wedding, **turning water into wine** *for everyone to drink. You can see the servants pouring it from jugs, over on the right."*

"Thanks SO much, Jesus. Because of all the fuss and attention over that miracle, we're forever known as the bad wedding hosts who didn't buy enough drink for their guests. So embarrassing!"

"But it IS pretty special that our wedding story is in the **Bible***, of all places. And, hey, it's a day none of our guests will forget in a hurry!"*

VIP-arty

"I have to say, apart from being pushed out of the spotlight, I do LOVE what Veronese has done with our painting."

*"Me too, darling! See, he imagined our ancient wedding as a lavish **16th-century banquet in Venice**, Italy—the time and place where he lived. SO glamorous. Just look at the beautiful, bright colors and patterns of people's clothes. And we're all having **so much fun**!"*

"So many VIPs, we're honored! I'd roll out a red carpet, but I don't want to hide that GORGEOUS tiled floor."

Big is beautiful

"Darling, do you know what the biggest painting in the Louvre is? Any ideas? You may find that all the other paintings look quite small. That's because **we are HUGE**, darling! Our painting is taller than a typical two-story house. WE are the biggest painting in the Louvre!"

*"How exciting! No wonder Veronese put **so much detail** into every one of us—the expression on each face, who people are talking to, even the shiny drapes of our clothes!"*

"Yes, these big, colorful paintings were Veronese's speciality . . . and people loved them! No cliches of the starving, unappreciated artist for Veronese—he had **PLENTY** of success while he was alive to enjoy it."

Napoleon's nerve

"You know, darling, I sometimes forget we've lived anywhere other than here."

*"Well, we HAVE been at the Louvre for **well over 200 years** now! Ever since . . ."*

". . . Yes, dear. Ever since Napoleon beat Venice in battle in 1798 and forced its leaders to take us down off the wall of that lovely monastery, and hand us over to his men."

"Exactly. Sorry, darling. Am I repeating myself?"

"We have been married for almost 500 years— it's to be expected!"

"True! I have to say, taking a country's prized works of art once you've beaten them in a war does seem like a shocking thing to do. It used to happen a lot, do you remember? In our case, King Louis XVIII did offer the people of Venice another painting in exchange—it was by Louis XIV's court painter, Le Brun."

"Well, let's look on the bright side—at least Napoleon sent us to the Louvre, where lots of people can come and admire us, instead of hiding us away in a private collection. Our fabulous party deserves to be seen by millions, darling!"

Spot the dog

"I don't remember saying on the invitation that dogs were welcome. Do you, darling?"

"Certainly not! I was so annoyed about the musicians bringing their little white hounds."

"And what about cats? Cats?! What kind of a person **brings a cat to a wedding**?"

"There are actually quite a few uninvited animal guests at our wedding feast . . ."

"Excuse me, dear reader. Yes, you there! You wouldn't mind looking for any dogs or cats around here, would you? **Thank you kindly**. Make sure to check under the tables!"

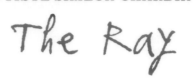

JEAN BAPTISTE SIMÉON CHARDIN (1699–1779)

The Ray

around 1725–1726   Oil paint on canvas

Jean Baptiste Siméon Chardin was a French painter who worked in Paris in the
18th century. He is known for his still lifes and paintings of everyday domestic scenes.

A fishy fright

Mreeoooaaw!! Ugh, that creepy, ghosty fish still makes me jump. You would have thought it'd be a kitten's DREAM, wouldn't you, being let loose on a table **full of fish and oysters**? But look at me, I'm a nervous wreck! My ears are pressed back, my back is arched, and my fur is standing on end—it looks like I've had an **electric shock**. Do I look happy to you?!

I'll admit, sometimes I feel sorry for the ray— even though it **grosses me out**. The fish and oysters in front of me are dead, too, but I don't feel much about them at all. Other than kind of **hungry**, once the shock has worn off . . .

I think it's the ray's face, you know. It's sort of **human and alien** at the same time, right? Its nostrils look like eyes and it's got that big human-ish mouth. And the pale, pearly skin makes it look all **otherworldly**, but where it's torn open you can see all the **real**, raw, squishy, complicated stuff inside. How does it make you feel, looking at the ray?

still-life star

Why, out of everything in the world, would Chardin choose to paint a random bunch of stuff on a table? Especially when, in his time, many people thought a painting of objects— a "**still life**"—could never be as good as a painting of famous people or ancient tales?

I bet Chardin knew that these rules were silly. He painted **so exceptionally** that people respected still lifes more, rather than respecting him less for painting them!

The best way to see how perfectly Chardin **balanced** everything is to cover parts with your hand (or paw, in my case). Those sticky-out knife and spoon handles, the oysters, even ME (gasp!). Just doesn't look right, does it?

The Valpinçon Bather

1808   Oil paint on canvas

Jean-Auguste-Dominique Ingres was a French painter who worked in the 19th century.
He was a technically skilled artist and worked in the Neoclassical style.

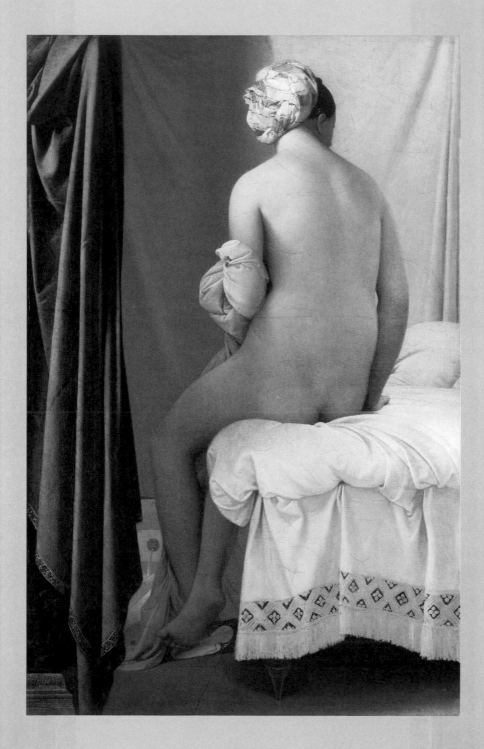

Do you MIND?! Here I am, preparing for a **lovely, soothing bath**, and people keep sneaking up behind me! Hardly relaxing.

It's not even that I mind baring my behind to the world; that's fine with me! It's just that a bath is supposed to be a **quiet, private** place to drift away from the world for a while. Don't you think? I mean, my bathtub probably looks different to yours—see, it's sunken into the floor by my bed, with a **little gold lion** spitting water into it. But the idea's the same, even 200+ years later!

It's extra unfair because so many people say how **relaxing** they find it to look at my painting. Is that how it makes you feel? I can totally see how. Some paintings are jam-packed full of STUFF: bright colors, patterns, people, objects, and details everywhere you look. But here it's just me, a bed, a curtain, and a **bathtub**.

And the really relaxing part, I suppose, is that I'm not trying to look any particular way. My body isn't squished and stretched into strange, unnatural, "feminine" shapes, or stuck in a pose that would be really weird and uncomfortable to hold in real life. **I'm just sitting here**, kind of slumped, waiting for my bath to run. Now, if you'll excuse me . . .

A pop of color

Between you and me, if Ingres wasn't so clever, this painting would be a **snoozefest**. In fact, it even took art critics years to go from feeling "meh" to "wow!" about it.

So what makes it a masterpiece? For me, two things. First up: the **red**. See how my head-wrap gives a pop of color at the top? Can you spot the other two pops of red? Next up, **texture**. Look at the bed, the fabrics, my pale skin. They show light and shadow, smooth and rough, folds and flows. Can you imagine what they'd **FEEL** like?

JUDITH LEYSTER (AROUND 1609–1660)

The Carousing Couple

1630   Oil paint on wood

Judith Leyster was a Dutch painter. She is one of the few women artists of the Dutch Golden Age. She is known for painting lively scenes of everyday merriment.

How about a sing-song?

"Dang, aren't there are a lot of serious faces around here! No wonder everyone goes on and on about Mona Lisa's little **smile**—must be a shock to see a famous painting crack one at all . . ."

"Ha! You're not wrong there, honey. Honestly, the side-eye we get just for me **playing a piece of music** and us singing a few songs. I mean, yeah, we might keep it up pretty late sometimes . . . but who doesn't love a party?!"

"And it's in our nature to be kind of **loud and lively**—that's what 'carousing' means, after all! Judith Leyster, who painted us, she LOVED showing musicians and people having fun."

"She was quite something, our Judith. There weren't many **women artists** back in her time, about 400 years ago. Especially ones who weren't even born into artist families. Judith's family made beer!"

"But she won people's respect all right. She even ran **her own studio**, with assistants and students. And she made the women in her paintings just as **confident** as she was. See, I'm not stuck in a corner like some fragile doll—I'm having fun!"

"Cheers to that! Now, how about another song?"

Leyster or Hals?

"Well, for hundreds of years, everyone said we were painted by **another artist**, Frans Hals. Our Judith knew him—in fact, she once sued him for stealing her assistant! And she might have studied with him. But it turned out his signature on the painting was a **fake**, covering up Judith's!"

"Yeah, an expert here at the Louvre discovered the forgery—good job! And then everyone realized that quite a few paintings that people had said were made by Hals or by Judith's husband were ACTUALLY made by Judith."

"It was great to see her get credit again. Shall we sing a little song to celebrate?!"

Stela of Nefertiabet

2590–2533 BCE   Painted limestone

This stone slab comes from the tomb of an ancient Egyptian princess from the
3rd millennium BCE. That's around the time when the Great Pyramid of Giza was built.

All these little pictures are like **magical promises** of food for me. In ancient Egypt, we believed that when someone died they simply moved to the **afterlife**, which was pretty similar to the living world. So in the afterlife, we would still need everything that made our life on Earth comfortable—food, drink, clothes, all our favorite things and little luxuries.

And writing or drawing things—including people—was like a spell or prayer to make them exist **forever**. Cool, right? So when I died, my family had artists create this feast-filled stela (stone slab) and put it in my family tomb. Mmmm . . .

To understand just how huge and splendid my feast is, you really need to read the hieroglyphs—the little pictures that we ancient Egyptians use as writing. Let's have a lesson!

OK, so see how by the tips of my beauteous toes there's a funny little drawing that looks like a half-inflated balloon on the end of a dagger? Well, that's a lotus plant, and that hieroglyph means 1,000. So wherever you see that drawing, it means I get 1,000 of whatever is nearby. **Thousands of tasty treats** just for me! How many lotus symbols can you spot?

The two panels above my table show all sorts, including delectable figs, cake, jujube fruit, and grown-up drinks made of grapes and dates. Will I share? **NO!** It's too rich for non-royals, sweetie.

A feast fit for a princess

Oh yummy! Mommy and Daddy did always say that I deserve **only the best,** and I agree. I am a princess, after all. But my artists really have outdone themselves. Just look at this feast! And it's **all mine**, for all eternity.

That's fifteen loaves of bread on the table in front of me. Perhaps I should start with one or two of those? Or three, why not?! And look, a delicious leg of meat above the bread—ox or antelope or something. And a goose, a little to the right. See? I'll admit, our ancient Egyptian way of drawing isn't **super-realistic**—often it's more like a code—but it still makes my mouth water!

Looking good!

I like to stay humble and all, but I'm not going to pretend I'm not fabulous. I mean, look at me, darling! I'm 4,500 years old and **still stylish as ever.** The wig of thick, black hair? Iconic. The leopardskin dress? Well, I wouldn't wear a new one, what with you modern people making the poor animals endangered and all, but this one's vintage chic!

I love the pose the artist has me in. So elegant! And before you start saying that I look all **twisty and odd**, that's just how people were usually drawn in my time. Head to the side, shoulders to the front, legs from the side. Not SUPER-comfy, but I've gotten used to it. Try it yourself!

Do you know I'm sometimes called "The Beauty of the East?" Blush. But what's important is **feeling good in myself**, not other people's opinions. That's what I try to remember when Mona Lisa gets all the attention, despite having NONE of my royal glamour. And know what really helps? Self-care, sweetie! The hieroglyphs in the top middle panel are for my incense, lotion and two kinds of eyeliner (green and black). Oh, I do **love to be pampered**!

And I've had a LITTLE help with staying so fresh and colorful, too. Basically, my stela was trapped **inside a wall** for thousands of years! I wouldn't recommend it—yes, it kept me in great condition but it was SO boring. Now I get to people-watch all day. Bliss!

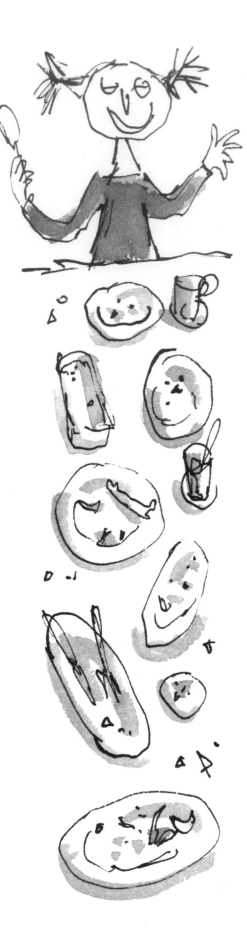

Haves and have-nots

So I'm not sure if I've mentioned that **I'm a princess**? Oh, I have? Well, it's kind of a big deal! It's written right above my head—my name, and that I'm part of Pharaoh Khufu's family. Probably his daughter, maybe his sister? Things get foggy after a few thousand years. Anyway, I was born into the **top of society**. Lots of money, power, servants, and luxury. Your classic princess life.

But at the other end of things, the poor end, I hear life was quite hard. Most people were farmers and worked **long days in the fields** trying to get enough food to eat and sell. Those people didn't get big, fancy burials like I did, but we know a little about their lives from art made for royals and other rich people.

Like this painting from a chapel that was part of a dedication to a man called Wensu, who was a scribe (yes, like the man on page 43!). Because Wensu's job was keeping count of grain harvests, the artist painted some scenes of people working in the fields. We even get a snapshot of their **work chatter**—see the hieroglyphs around them?

I do feel sorry for them—look at their plain outfits and how busy and bent-backed they are. It must be nice to feel useful, though. Without their hard work, I wouldn't have any yummy bread to eat. But seeing how most people lived does make me feel lucky—and **a little guilty.** What's that? NO, I still won't share my feast! How dare you!

EUGÈNE DELACROIX (1798–1863)

Liberty Leading the People

1830   Oil paint on canvas

Eugène Delacroix was a French painter who worked during the 19th century. He was famous for large, colorful, Romantic scenes from history and literature.

What do I think of Mona Lisa? I *don't* think of her—I've got a **revolution** to lead! My name is Liberty, and I'm all about freedom. **Freedom for all,** freedom for always! That's why I'm leading this rowdy rabble in Paris's "July Revolution" against the king.

Is it hard work? Yes! Do I sometimes get chilly out here and question my clothing choices? Yes! But people can **change the world** when they have something to believe in, and I know that my destiny is to be that something.

Funnily enough, Delacroix didn't consider himself much of a revolutionary. However, seeing others fight inspired him to create this world-famous painting. And, in turn, it has inspired people to **fight for freedom** for almost 200 years. See, there's always more than one way to change the world!

Red, white, and blue

Recognize the flag I'm proudly waving? That's right, it's **French**! But back when Delacroix painted me, this was a dangerous revolutionary symbol. It stood for a France without kings, where PEOPLE had more power. Obviously, the French king wasn't a big fan . . .

Can you spot the other patches of **red, white, and blue** that Delacroix dotted around the painting? The flag and its colors are like an idea in visible form. Kind of like me! I'm not a real person exactly—I'm the **idea** of freedom in the shape of a person. I'm revolution come to life!

stop biting my butt!

Owwwwww!!!! Come on, Lion, give it a rest! Honestly, after 350 years, you'd think he'd get bored of all this **biting**—or at least tired out. Anyway, hello, my name's Milo . . . and you're not exactly seeing me at my best. Did you ever have **a bad day** that just kept getting worse? Yeah, me too—that's how I got into this mess.

I started the day as one of the world's greatest athletes, famous through ancient Greece and beyond as a wrestler and multiple Olympic Games winner. But the story goes that I then declared I could split a tree stump in half **with my bare hands**. Well, spoiler: I couldn't. Can you work out what happened next?

Yeah, I got my hand stuck. NOT the cool, impressive look I was going for. And as I was trying to laugh it off, **wild beasts** came and gobbled me up! Like I said, bad day. And now my most embarrassing moment is carved into a world-famous statue for eternity. Ouch.

On the plus side, I look pretty buff, right? All that writhing and twisting in pain really shows off my muscles! Puget even smoothed and polished my marble skin, leaving everything else rough, to show them off better. The man was a **marble genius**! Even he said, "The marble trembles before me." Hmm, sounds kind of vain—but I'm one to talk!

Baroque-ing out

My story is pretty dramatic, right? Pretty intense? That's how Puget knew it would be a perfect fit for his Baroque style. See, Baroque was an art movement that spread across Europe about 400 years ago, and it was all about bringing the DRAMA.

See how Lion and I look like we could **spring to life** at any moment, from our thrown-back heads and taut muscles down to our gripping toes? How you can almost hear me crying out? Baroque was all about capturing that real physical and emotional **power** to make people lose themselves in art and actually FEEL something.

The Seated Scribe

around 2620–2500 BCE   Limestone, alabaster, rock crystal, and copper

We don't know the names of any ancient Egyptian artists.
This statue was found at Saqqara, an ancient burial ground in Egypt.

You know, it's never bothered me that Mona Lisa gets more attention than the rest of us. Honestly! I've been around a long time—around 4,500 years, if we're counting—so frankly I'm just happy not to have **crumbled away** into dust. It's very flattering that so many people want to come and see me at all, especially given that I'm not a great leader or a god or anything fancy.

Just a scribe, that's me, dedicated to serving my pharaoh (that's what we called the king or queen back in my day) by keeping written records and managing the kingdom's everyday goings-on. I've still got my **trusty scroll** laid out in my lap, although I seem to remember having a brush at some point, too . . . Ah well, things are bound to go missing over the years.

If I ever allow myself one little complaint, it's only this—**I love my work**, really I do, but I've been on scribe duty for thousands of years now. Would it be **too much** to ask for a day off?!

Look into my eyes

People always tell me—or, rather, tell each other in front of me—how lifelike I look. **"Those eyes!"** they gasp. "That collarbone, that soft little belly, those creases and shadows around the mouth, cheeks, and chin. And the fingernails—look, you can even see the cuticles." Of course, I can't take credit for any of that—and neither can the artist who made me, because nowadays no one's sure who it was!

They were obviously **very skilled** at carving stone, though, and they went to lots of trouble over my eyes. Look closely—the whites are made from a red-veined stone so they're extra realistic, and the crystals set in the center are polished so they **catch the light** like human eyes. Almost spooky, right? Boo!

CONSTANCE MAYER (OR MAYER-LAMARTINIÈRE) (1778–1821)

The Dream of Happiness

1819   Oil paint on canvas

Constance Mayer was a French painter who worked in the 19th century.
She is known for her peaceful portraits and scenes of family life.

Dozers and dreamers

"Miss! Hey, miss, excuse me!" She never answers me back, you know—too busy looking at those three down at the other end of the boat.

I mean, come on, I'm the one with wings! That makes me way more interesting than them, right? Even our artist wanted people to look at me. See how she painted my face all brightly lit up, like I'm under a spotlight?

OK, yeah, snoozy mom and baby are in the light, too . . . and even dreamy-eyed dad has a touch of it. But they wouldn't be snuggled together so **happily** if it wasn't for me. See, I'm Love. And that silent, staring lady in front of me is Fortune—so they owe a lot to her, too.

Our painter knew how important **love and luck** were to being happy. Life can be hard and cruel sometimes, and it often was to her. She tried to follow her dreams of working as an artist and living happily with the man she loved, a famous artist called Pierre-Paul Prud'hon, but she had a really rough time.

See, the world can put itself in the way of people's dreams. But that's why great art can be so magical—it doesn't obey the world's rules. The world beyond this boat, with all its dark lands and deep waters, can't touch this family and their **perfect happiness**. The most Mayer lets it do is blow around a scarf or two in the breeze. That's what makes this painting a dream, but a beautiful one.

Twinsies!

So the Louvre has a sketch by Pierre-Paul Prud'hon that will look VERY familiar if you've seen our painting . . . . Is it a fake? A coincidence? Or cheating, like when someone in class copies your math homework (or you copy theirs, hmm)? **Trick question**—it's none of those things!

Prud'hon and Mayer actually worked together, so she used his sketch as a starting point for her painting. Many people at the time thought women couldn't be artists, and said that Mayer was just a kind of paint-by-numbers copyist for Prud'hon. But now we know she was **an exceptional artist** in her own right, and we say "Boooooo!" to those sexists!

45

GUILLAUME COUSTOU (1677–1746)

The Marly Horses

1745 Marble

Guillaume Coustou was a French sculptor who worked during the Baroque period. He is known for his dramatic works, many of which were made for French kings.

WOOOOAAAAHHH THERE!

*"GET OFF ME! I am a WILD BEAST, a free spirit who cannot be tamed! Especially not by some **half-naked human** who hasn't even brought me a carrot or a nice crunchy apple."*

"YEAH, SAME! It's like, grab some snacks for me and some clothes for yourself, then we'll talk. I mean, he's my groom, he's supposed to be at WORK right now. And I'm practically wearing more than he is, with this shaggy rug on my back!"

"If I were our grooms, I'd be much more afraid of us. Look how POWERFUL we are! Twice as tall as your average human, muscles bulging from head to hoof, heads thrown back with flowing manes and open mouths as we cry out in fury . . . ."

"Neeiiiggghhhhhhh!! Yeah, those grooms should **watch themselves**. We've already managed to break the straps they're trying to hold us by."

*"Exactly! If we weren't made of this heavy marble, we'd be OFF. Just imagine us galloping through Paris, side by side—how **impressive** we'd look. Can you picture it?"*

"Oooohh yeah! Although we're pretty impressive anywhere, to be fair. Hard to believe our sculptor, Coustou, carved us each out of a giant block of marble, ten feet high, along with everything around us—our groom, rug, plants and . . . rocks. OK, so maybe that last one is more believable."

Right at home

*"You know, as **wild and free-spirited** as I am, I do really enjoy being in this Marly Courtyard place. It's like being outside but with a glass roof over my head so I'm nice and cozy. Do you think I'm getting old, talking like that?"*

"That's OK, we're both getting old! It was fun being in the grounds of the Château de Marly—nice touch from Louis XV to put us either side of a drinking trough for horses! And I loved being in that big square, the Place de la Concorde, during the first French Revolution—it felt like we were part of something. But we were getting so worn and chilly with all the wind and rain on us."

*"Yeah, maybe we can be **wild, free, AND cozy** all at once? Uh-oh, I really do sound old!"*

47

THÉODORE GÉRICAULT (1791–1824)

The Raft of the Medusa

1818–1819   Oil paint on canvas

Théodore Géricault was a French painter and draftsman during the Romantic period.
He is famous for depicting dramatic scenes of real events that happened during his lifetime.

"STOP! Wait! Where are you going? We're over heeeerreee!! Look, this way, can't you see us? My arm's aching from waving this red-and-white flag, and I don't know how much longer I can balance on these barrels . . ."

"Uggghh! More than 200 years now and he still thinks that dot of a ship on the horizon is going to come and pick us up. I keep telling everyone, it's **too far away**! I mean, can you even see it? The ghostly little gray mast poking up out of the water and into the sky, just by the armpit of the guy in the red shorts? (A **very stinky armpit**—we've been on this raft forever . . .)"

"At least I'm TRYING! What good are you doing sulking over there under that red blanket, like the world's oldest, grumpiest Little Red Riding Hood impersonator?"

"Um, actually I think you'll find that I'm thinking **very deeply** about death and humanity. Oh, and how we're all ultimately powerless against the mighty forces of nature, fate, and the cruel indifference of our supposed leaders."

"Yeah, well, everyone thinks you're a real downer. We're ALL stranded and starving, not just you—and that's those of us who are lucky enough to still be alive! See how the rest of us survivors are looking up, stretching out, facing the ship or each other, **trying our very hardest** to LIVE? Ugh. When we do get rescued by that ship, there's no way I'm sharing a bunk with YOU."

"Now, I bet you're thinking that this nightmarish raft scene is from a story, or just something Géricault made up. (Artists can be SO dramatic, right?!) But no. The Medusa was an actual ship, with a fancy, useless captain who only got his job through having rich, powerful friends. He hadn't even sailed a ship for twenty years!"

"The Medusa ended up crashing. And, predictably, it wasn't prepared with enough lifeboats. So we quickly made this **flimsy raft** for everyone without a lifeboat seat . . ."

". . . and the captain apparently cut our raft loose! Left us for dead to make sure HE got home safely. Coward or what?! We started as 150 on this raft. Guess how many of us made it back and survived long enough to tell the tale? . . . TEN."

Romantic? Really?

"In my day, romance was flowers and a nice dinner. But apparently this painting of our **misery and suffering** is Romantic with a capital R?"

*"That's right, Géricault was a massive Romantic. But Romantic art doesn't mean corny Valentine's cards and cuddly bears holding hearts. Back in Géricault's day, it was a **new way** of thinking about and making art. Breaking the strict rules that told people how to think, live, and create—and working out your OWN, more free ways of doing things, by thinking and feeling deeply."*

"Ah, so I'm not the only deep thinker and feeler. What else was this Romantic art about?"

*"Nature played a BIG part in it. See all the color and movement in the sky and the sea? It's not just a still backdrop for humans. **It's ALIVE.** You can almost SEE the wind as it pushes the sail, blows the dark clouds, churns the water, and lifts the waves. It's complex and dramatic."*

"So is all this Romantic rebellion why Géricault painted us so big, even though we're ordinary people who happened to make the news? Because, if I remember, big paintings were only supposed to show long-ago history, ancient myths or Bible stories. Not **regular joes** caught in big scandals only a couple of years before . . ."

"That's right! And lots of critics did NOT approve."

Big and bold

*"You can't tell this from a book but our painting is HUGE. Like, half the size of an average movie theater screen. **SERIOUS wow factor**! Géricault worked from sunrise to sunset for eight months to finish it. And when it was first shown, at the Louvre, it caused a stir as massive as us. I still remember the gasping and pointing . . ."*

"Me, too. I think lots of people found the **gruesome dead bodies** and the rawness of our suffering kind of hard to take—especially at such a huge size. It's pretty shocking stuff, even now. And that's from someone holding a corpse!"

"Géricault went out of his way to make the scene, and the bodies, as realistic as possible. Pretty obsessive! He interviewed survivors, visited the morgue to study dead bodies, recreated the raft in his studio from a survivor's drawing, and even drew real body parts to get the sickly colors and lifeless poses just right."

"And he did it without anyone asking or paying for it, which was **really unusual.** He KNEW it was special . . . It fired up the *Medusa* scandal more than ever, and really stirred up protests against France's king—and our elitist society that made poor people suffer so a few could stay rich."

"That's right. Even though people already knew the gory details—including ones that our painting doesn't even show, like cannibalism (yup, seriously) . . . seeing the story in a painting made it hit people harder."

Video star

"We don't worry about Mona Lisa because we're also a BIG DEAL. Jay-Z and Beyoncé even chose to stand in front of **us**, too, when they shot a music video at the Louvre."

"Um, you should think WAY harder about why that might be. When the Medusa crashed, it was on its way to take control of Senegal, in West Africa. So some people think Géricault used the painting to criticize slavery and colonialism. There was only one surviving Black sailor recorded, but Géricault painted three of us. Also, I'm at the top of the pyramid of bodies on the raft—you HAVE to look at me, see that I'm suffering, hoping, trying, and being let down, too."

Monzon Lion

around 1100–1300 Bronze
Originally from Monzón de Campos, Spain

In the 12th and 13th centuries, the south of Spain was Muslim, and ruled by
a caliph (a historical Islamic religious ruler) based in the city of Córdoba.
This lion was an ornament on a fountain at a grand palace.

Don't call me a big mouth!

Honestly, some people's manners . . . the pointing, the laughing, the impressions! YES, **my mouth is huge**. It's a train tunnel, it's a yawning whale, it's a dark cavern and a megaphone and a black hole that belongs deep in outer space. OK?! But, as I keep trying to explain to everyone, it's big for a REASON.

That reason is: I'm not just any old lion, I'm a **fountain**! Well, a spout of a fountain, really. I can't remember, but apparently people think I was one of twelve lion-shaped spouts. I was discovered around 150 years ago at Monzón de Campos in Spain (hence the Monzon part of my name), in the ruins of a once-great castle fortress. Then I joined the art collection of a world-famous Spanish painter called Mariano Fortuny. Pretty glamorous for an old fountain, right?

But obviously **I'm functional, too**. See that big, round hole in my belly? That's where I connected up to a water duct, so the water came rushing up through my neck and out of my terrifically big mouth. Imagine **how impressive** I must have looked! Stocky and proud, shining and steady-footed, pouring forth a glittering jet of clear, cool water. Can't you just see it?

Patterns and positivity

Have you noticed the patterns engraved all over me? Pretty, right? I'm quite proud of them, TBH, because it's really rare for a metal artwork as old as I am (at least 700 years old, if you can believe it) to have survived at all. Let alone in such **amazing condition**— if I say so myself!

Islamic works of art often have patterns like mine, with shapes, leaves, flowers and words all weaving together. And the words engraved on me in Kufic, one of the oldest written forms of Arabic, wish people "complete happiness" and "perfect blessing." Well, couldn't we all use some of that good stuff?

JOHANNES VERMEER (1632–1675)

The Lacemaker

around 1669–1670 Oil paint on canvas mounted on wood

Johannes Vermeer was a Dutch painter who lived and worked during the Dutch Golden Age. He is famous for the precision of his painting and his beautifully lit, realistic scenes of everyday life.

Lost in Lace

Oh, hello there! Please do excuse me for keeping my eyes on my work. It's so tricky if you get mixed up, and I'm making pretty good progress today! Really "**in the zone**," as you say nowadays, or so I hear.

Do you ever get that "in the zone" feeling when you're doing something creative, like painting or writing? Where it suddenly feels easier and you enjoy it a lot more, and it's not exactly relaxing but it's like it fills up your whole brain? It's a great feeling, isn't it?

Well, when I get in a good rhythm with my lacemaking (which involves criss-crossing and twisting threads to create lovely shapes), that's just how I feel. Like I'm in **perfect control** and my work is flowing nicely into the world. And that's just how Vermeer painted me. See how my whole body is focused on my work, from my tilted head and my curled-over shoulders to my hands poised with taut threads? But I don't look tense or stressed, do I? Just peacefully lost in my work.

Now, although I'm a **tiny** painting (smaller than a sheet of letter paper!), without much exciting action, I have a LOT of fans. Why? Well, I think Vermeer's done something special here, capturing this moment. It doesn't matter who I am, or what my life might look like in the past or the future. The rest of the world falls away and I'm just a person, hard at work, trying to bring something beautiful into the world.

Lights, Camera, Lacemaker!

Can you see the tiny pale dots of light scattered across my collar, over my work, and through the spilling threads and fabric to my side? And speaking of threads, see how **they're all blurry**, almost as if you're looking at a photo that's too close-up to be in focus, while my hands and face are clearly lit and shadowed?

Vermeer put a lot of thought and work into my painting, playing around with light. Some people think he experimented with a camera obscura, an early form of a camera, to come up with these effects. If you feel like you're sitting right next to me, that's on purpose. If my hands are the first thing you see, that's on purpose, too!

Art and craft

Vermeer was kind of a genius at using paint to create **exactly** the effect he wanted. And that doesn't just *happen*, you know. It takes a lot of hard work, learning and time-perfecting skills. This "craft" side of art might not be as glamorous as the big ideas and the flashes of inspiration and the frantic splashing of paint, but for Vermeer it was just as important.

For instance, being an expert in the craft of painting meant Vermeer knew just how to use COLOR. So what might be **deadly dull** in someone else's hand comes to life in his. Look at the wall behind me—pretty shabby, right? If Vermeer wanted his painting to "pop," or look a little prettier, couldn't he have made it a nice, rich color?

But no! Because without the dullness of the wall, my yellow dress doesn't catch your eye and put your gaze where it needs to be. Well, couldn't my dress just be brighter? No! Because then the deep blue of the pillow couldn't chop through the yellow so clearly, creating the front part of the painting. See?

I've always thought that perhaps Vermeer painted me and my work so respectfully because he saw us as **fellow creators**. While others might dismiss my lacemaking as just "craft," far beneath the lofty heights of "art," maybe Vermeer—who so respected the importance and difficulty of craft in his own work—valued it in mine, too. I do hope so.

Modest me

Some paintings are simply STUFFED full of symbols and settings that tell you all sorts of things about their subjects. But not mine! What can you actually tell about me from looking at my painting?

I mean, I make lace—obviously; I'm dressed (and hairdressed) neatly and modestly; I've got what's probably a Bible or prayer book in front of me. All of these things point to me being a "nice young lady," and lacemaking was a very appropriate activity for Dutch ladies. So you know **I'm not exactly a rebel grrrl** (or at least a very secret one).

And yes, maybe it is kind of "eye roll" that Vermeer seems to be praising me for being a nice, modest young lady doing what's expected of me. But he's also **showing respect** for my work, even though it's a traditionally "feminine" art, and he's putting me and my creativity centerstage. Hey, things aren't always 100% good or bad, right?

Home is where the art is

Did you know that Vermeer's father, Reynier, made fabric for a living? Not lace, but something called caffa—a mix of silk and cotton or wool. There's a good chance Vermeer may have seen his father at work. Later on, Reynier became an art dealer—so art and craft were always **woven** into Vermeer's life.

Why don't you try looking at your life like Vermeer? What familiar things and everyday actions are beautiful if you stop to look at them?

Sarcophagus of the spouses

around 520–510 BCE Painted terracotta

Found in Cerveteri, Italy

The Etruscan people lived in what is now central Italy. Etruscan artists created some very distinctive artworks, often influenced by Greek art. Cerveteri was an important site where lots of archaeological finds have been discovered, including sarcophaguses (or coffins) like this one.

"Do you know what's even better than lounging around on a comfy, cushioned bed? Eating a **huge, delicious meal** while you're doing it!"

*"Woo, I'll second that! Seriously, the way we're posed is how aristocratic (rich and fancy) Etruscans like us used to eat our dinner at great banquets. And the BEST part: I was **just as important** a guest as my lovely husband."*

"Yes, we've heard that lots of cultures over time have had VERY SILLY ideas about women not being as good or important as men. But my wonderful wife and I were **equals** in life, just as we are now in the afterlife."

"Ah, if only we had a big plate of cakes to chomp through, like we used to at those banquets . . ."

Sappy spouses

"All this fuss about lovely Mona Lisa stealing everyone's spotlight . . . what nonsense! We're happy, aren't we, my dear wife? Comfy bed, plump pillows and an **eternity spent in each other's arms**. What more could we want?"

*"Too true, sweetheart. We're grateful that our families, and the creators they hired to make our sarcophagus, set us up for a wonderful afterlife together. See, our people—the Etruscans, from what you now call Italy— believed that **life didn't end with death.** The ashes of our bodies are safely hidden inside this sarcophagus-bed we're lying on, and our spirits live on in our portraits—as the hopeless romantics we've always been."*

Cleopatra Disembarking at Tarsus

around 1642–1643   Oil paint on canvas

Claude Gellée—known as Claude Lorrain, because he came from the province of Lorraine—was a 17th-century French artist. He is famous for his landscape paintings showing scenes from history and mythology.

Excuse me, I'm the star!

It's an absolute OUTRAGE, that's what it is. **This is supposed to be MY painting**, it's got MY name in the title, and just look! Can you even tell which tiny little ant-person I am? I am the queen of ancient Egypt, for heaven's sake. I'm a legend, I'm an icon, William SHAKESPEARE wrote a play about me. And here I am, being upstaged by the stupid sky!

I mean, yes, it's a very nice sky. The little painter man, Claude something, was pretty good at skies. And water, and sunlight. I mean, they were his whole THING, really. Making nature the subject, rather than the background— that's what Claude was all about. **Quite the rebel** in his time, I hear.

See how the sun is the only point of light in the painting? And how everything has a hazy, calm, evening look, all soft yellow light and long shadows? (Shadows that thrust me so RUDELY into this murky half-light.) It makes me think about how we're all just existing within nature, living our little lives beside the big sea and beneath the wide sky, totally dependent on the huge, shining sun beyond our world.

Quite a beautiful reminder, really, isn't it? But still no excuse for the INSULT of **stealing my spotlight.** I mean, how can I draw as big a crowd as Mona Lisa when people can't even see my face?!

Rome and reality

If you squint, or get out a magnifying glass, can you take a guess at what's going on in my painting? Tricky, but it's actually some VERY important history in action. This is the moment when I arrived at Tarsus, which was part of the Roman Empire, and met my future hubbie, Mark Antony. Our marriage **literally changed history**, by uniting ancient Rome and Egypt! Talk about the original power couple . . .

Tarsus didn't really look like this, though. That Claude man liked to put ancient stories and buildings into his paintings, mixed in with scenes from his present time—like the Rome he saw and loved on vacation. And the whole landscape got a poetic, dramatic lift. It's pretty and all, but I'm still too FURIOUS to really care.

GIUSEPPE ARCIMBOLDO (1527–1593)

Summer

1573   Oil paint on canvas

Giuseppe Arcimboldo was an Italian painter. He lived and worked during the Renaissance period, and is famous for his portraits composed of fruits, vegetables, and other objects.

Fruity face

Anyone else getting a real whiff of cucumber? Ooh, and some cherry! Nice. Hmm, maybe some pea and pear in there, too? Delicious. Oh wait, haha, **I'm smelling myself again**! I know I might look kind of odd to you, but I feel and smell wonderful. I'm simply BURSTING with life in all its ripe, colorful, beautifully varied glory!

How many different fruits and vegetables can you count in my face? Go on, try it, it's fun! You can even grab a friend or family member and make it a game. Don't forget my peachy cheeks, my darling little eggplant ear and my GORGEOUS artichoke brooch.

And I tell you what, if you enjoyed yourselves, look up the other paintings in my set: *Spring*, *Autumn* and *Winter*. Arcimboldo cleverly made up their faces from all sorts of natural goodies from their times of year, too. We work together perfectly, just like the seasons—and the stages of life.

See, humans are **part of nature**, too . . . as much as modern cities and fast cars and shiny plastic-wrapped things might try to convince you otherwise. People grow and bloom and age and rejoin the Earth, just like any other living thing. I think old Arcimboldo was trying to remind people of that. What do you think?

Copycat

Now, I'm going to let you in on a secret . . . I'm a copy! Not a fake, now. I think of it as having lots of identical twins. Arcimboldo was no poor, misunderstood artist whose work didn't sell. Quite the opposite! I was a **SMASH HIT**. After Arcimboldo made his first *Summer* painting in 1563, people wanted more—and he kept going! I was made ten years later.

See, hiding in the weave of my wheat jacket is "Giuseppe Arcimboldo" (on the neck) and "1573" (on the shoulder). He also **mixed things up** so I'm not an exact copy. See the flowery frame painted around me? That's not in the original *Summer* at all!

The Winged Victory of Samothrace

around 220–185 BCE   Marble
Found in Samothrace, Greece

This statue, which stands over nine feet tall, was made in the early 2nd century BCE.
Its sculptor was probably famous in Greece but their name is now unknown. The sculpture
is one of the few Greek statues that has survived to the present day. It became
famous mostly through copies made by Roman sculptors.

A goddess restored

Hello down there, small and insignificant human. It is I, Nike, **goddess of VICTORY**! Are you quivering and bowing down in my presence? I'm sure you are, but without my head it's hard to tell.

Still, I'm very lucky to be in one piece—I used to be in **110 pieces**! Apparently I got smashed up in an earthquake or something. But I was rediscovered about 160 years ago and nicely restored to my present goddess-y glory.

Wind beneath my wings

Today, I feel just as strong, just as full of life and movement, as when I was first made—over 2,000 years ago. And I've been assured that, **even headless and armless**, I look as impressive as ever. I believe every word of it.

For a start, I'm enormous, one of the biggest ancient Greek statues ever found! Standing on the prow of my marble ship (that's the pointy part at the front, for any non-sailors), I tower over the very tallest people your puny human world has to offer. I am over nine feet tall!

And just LOOK at these wings! Thrust back into the wind, muscles and feathers poised to send me **soaring** through the sky. I may be carved of hard, still marble, but do you see how the cloth draped over me ripples and waves in the breeze? Aahhh, sometimes I swear I can still feel that wind rushing over me, hear the roaring sea, smell and taste the salty air.

See, when I was first created, I stood on a hilltop on the sunny Greek island of Samothrace, facing out to the sparkling ocean. I was made as a **gift to the gods**, to say thank you for a successful battle at sea, and I was placed where sailors could see me as they set out over the waves. Close your eyes. Can you imagine me there?

JEAN-ANTOINE WATTEAU (1684–1721)

Pierrot

around 1718–1719   Oil paint on canvas

Jean-Antoine Watteau was a French painter and draftsman. He was a master of the light and elegant Rococo style, and often made works based on Italian comedy, ballet, and theater.

The sad clown speaks

"Oh, hi there. Are you here to laugh at me, too? Sigh. Go on then, get it over with. What will you pick on first? My too-short pants? My dopey, daydreamy gaze? The big ruff around my neck? Look, I know how silly I look in this **floppy outfit**. But it's my fate to be ridiculous. Sigh.

For I am Pierrot, or Pedrolino if you want my original Italian name, and I was literally created to be the **butt of the joke**, and the target of pranks, and the guy who is always in love but never loved back. Sigh. See, I'm a character in the Commedia dell'Arte, a type of theater that was popular around 300 years ago—especially in Italy, where it came from, and France, where my painter came from.

See the people behind me? They're Commedia dell'Arte characters, too. Always teasing me or leaving me out. Sigh. They're probably whispering behind my back right now."

"OK, Pierrot, enough with the pity party."

"Ugh, who said that?! I don't know that voice!"

*"It's me, Donkey, by your foot. Yes, I can talk— this is a painting, and things are different here . . . Yes, the infuriating Doctor is still riding me. Yes, the red-suited Captain is still preening and boasting, although we all know he's a coward. Yes, the two lovers are still SUPER boring and annoying. But here, **you're the STAR!**"*

Listen to the donkey

*"So, Pierrot, listen up. The people of France loved YOU more than any other character. That's why Watteau put you **centerstage**. It's YOUR painting, it's YOUR place to shine. Look at the gleam on the silk of your white outfit, the soft and luxurious folds. Can you see how many shades Watteau used to get just the right effect? And did you know that the full-length pose Watteau put you in is traditionally used only for royals and VERY IMPORTANT leaders?*

*I think he saw something **heroic** in you. The other Commedia dell'Arte characters laugh at your honesty, innocence and hope, but **that's what makes you special**. It's why people love YOU best."*

JACQUES-LOUIS DAVID (1748–1825)

The Consecration of the Emperor Napoleon

1806–1807   Oil paint on canvas

Jacques-Louis David was a French artist. He worked in the Neoclassical style, and was famous for his paintings of ancient, historical, and contemporary scenes. He was Napoleon's favorite painter.

"SPLENDID, aren't I? Have you ever SEEN such a man, **such a spectacle**, such an array of rich, powerful, perfectly dressed people? Of course you haven't! (Especially not in that dull little Mona Lisa's painting.) For I am Napoleon I, great emperor of France, and I accept ONLY the best. So I chose good old Jacques to paint this world-changing moment when I stepped up to lead France.

What do you mean, you're not sure which one I am? Unbelievable! Yes, I admit there are a **lot of people** in my painting—191 apparently, although I'm far too busy to count them myself. And my painting is even more overwhelming in person, you know—it's FABULOUSLY huge.

OK, just look around the painting and notice if there's a spot that your eyes feel like they keep getting dragged back to. Is it at the foot of the middle pillar, to the right of the golden cross-on-a-stick? Aha, **there's my glorious face**! Bathed in light, one golden crown upon my head and another raised aloft in my hands as I crown my wife as empress.

See, Jacques was good at **directing eyes** where they should be—me! The crowds are facing me, obviously. But can you see how he's darkened the edges to make a sort of spotlight around me? And created diagonal lines, like the shadow in the top left, that point down towards me? Clever! Can you pick out other lines that do the same?"

"Did you hear what Napoleon's mom called me? A suck-up! After everything I've done for her son . . . I made him a **modern-day hero** in my paintings, a mighty emperor in the style of the ancient Greek and Roman leaders he admired so much.

Well, at least I know Napoleon appreciates my work—I was his official painter. I even took the liberty of painting myself in here, above Napoleon's mom and second on the left. See? Yes, the moody guy . . .

I also threw in someone who looks like ancient Roman leader Julius Caesar, gazing approvingly at him. I regret nothing! I **really believed** in the French republic that Napoleon led. I liked the idea of the people choosing our country's leader, rather than being stuck with kings and queens. And I wanted heroes in my art just as much as Napoleon wanted to be a hero!"

You brazen boy!

"That's QUITE enough from you now, Napoleon. Let someone else talk for a change! Your MOTHER, for a start, hmm?

Would you believe that my son told the artist to paint me into this scene, even though I DELIBERATELY chose not to attend in real life? You'll find me sitting on a big chair, in the bottom row between the two pillars, to the left of the golden cross-on-a-stick.

*I told Napoleon, I said, 'If you don't start being nicer to your brothers and give Lucien a special role in your empire, I won't come at all.' Well, I wasn't bluffing! Unfortunately, he can pay this suck-up painter to **indulge his ego** . . . I must admit, though, it is quite nice to have a front-row seat to see his big moment. He's my boy, after all."*

The time-traveling emperor

Hey, that was my job!

"Huh?! Where am I? Why is everyone dressed weird? Where are all the togas? This doesn't look like ancient Rome at all! I am Julius Caesar and I DEMAND to be told what's going on . . .

*. . . Aaahh, wait, I've just remembered. Sorry, sometimes takes me a sec. And now that I remember, I'm FURIOUS! This jumped-up Napoleon person who lived 2,000 years after me has shoved me in his painting (I'm just behind him, to the left of the big stick with the swirl on top), to make himself **look more important**!*

Apparently Napoleon saw himself as the kind of leader that I and my successor, Augustus, proved ourselves to be back in ancient Rome. Strong, ambitious, worthy of great power. Pretty confident, wasn't he?!"

"Hmm, interesting that our artist chose to paint Napoleon crowning his wife, rather than the moment of Napoleon becoming emperor. Because if he HAD shown what he first intended to, you would have seen Napoleon taking the crown from ME, the Pope, and crowning HIMSELF!

Can you believe it?! It's taken me a long time to get over the nerve of that, I tell you. When you're the leader of a religion (Catholicism, in my case), you get used to people following your lead and your traditions.

Still, at least I've had a comfy seat for the last 200 years. That's me in the throne at the front, raising my hand in a blessing. Hmmm. I've DEFINITELY never dreamed about tripping Napoleon up with my big metal stick . . ."

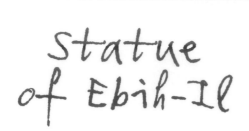

statue of Ebih-Il

around 2400 BCE   Alabaster, with lapis lazuli, shell, and bitumen

This statue was made in the 3rd millennium BCE and was found in the city of Mare, on the banks of the Euphrates river in modern-day Syria. It comes from the Sumerian civilization.

Look into my eyes . . .

Now, I know my starey blue eyes are **hypnotic**, but guess what? It's actually ME who's entranced!

The symbols scratched into the back of my shoulder say: "Ebih-Il, intendant, in adoration before the goddess Ishtar." The most helpful tattoo ever, right? It tells you all sorts of things: my name, my job, and what it is I'm supposed to be doing. And I was found in a temple dedicated to Ishtar, who my people (the ancient Sumerians) worshipped, so it all makes perfect sense!

Now can you see all the **love and wonder** in my face? How I look like somebody seeing the cutest puppy EVER? My artist took a lot of care in making me—maybe **my eyes** most of all. The white is made of shell, the blue is a semi-precious stone called lapis lazuli, and the thick black eyeliner around them is made of bitumen—that's the stuff roads are made from!

Kind of a big deal

I was **pretty important** back in my day, about 4,500 years ago. As an intendant, I helped run my city—Mari, a wonderful, wealthy place in what we called Mesopotamia. Sadly, Mari is no more. I was dug out of the ground about ninety years ago, in a place you now call Syria.

My artist showed I was a **big boss**. See how I'm sitting with my hands folded? My people usually only showed GODS like this, so it's a VERY big honor. Also, imagine the TIME the artist spent on me! My eyes, yes, but also carving my wavy beard, my chair of woven reeds and my shaggy animal-skin skirt. **All for me!** I'd blush if I could.

ÉLISABETH VIGÉE-LE BRUN (1755–1842)

Self-Portrait with Her Daughter Julie

1789   Oil paint on canvas

Élisabeth Vigée-Le Brun was a French painter who lived and worked in the 18th century, during the Neoclassical period. She was particularly famous for her portraits.

"Mooommmm, why do we have to wear these clothes?"

"Because we're being Neoclassical, darling. We're dressed kind of like we're in ancient Rome or Greece but also . . . um . . . not. It's a style that's a **mix of ancient times and today**. Quite fashionable in the art world, you know . . . On the other hand, the art world in our day often seemed to think that great art was only male artists painting other men doing 'manly' things. But you and I, women and girls, family—we're JUST as interesting and important."

"Oh, OK. Mooommmm, why do people care that we're SMILING?"

"Well, they don't any more, my love. But when I first painted us, nearly 250 years ago, it just wasn't done. People weren't used to it; they thought good art had to be SERIOUS and follow tradition. That meant **no smiles** with teeth showing!"

"Weird. Mooommmm, why did you leave the wall all bare and brown and BORING?"

"Thanks a lot! Well, because WE are what really matters. I love you and you love me, any place, any time. The rest is just background."

"OK. I love you, too. But I still think the wall should be RAINBOW colored."

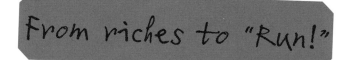

From riches to "Run!"

"Hard to believe that just a few months after I painted this, we had to **run for our lives** . . ."

"Mom, you're so DRAMATIC. We didn't run, we took our nice stuff and just lived abroad."

"Do I have to remind you what happened to our friend, queen Marie Antoinette? I was famous for being her favorite artist. And then . . ."

*". . . Ah yes, the French Revolution people didn't want a king or queen and they **chopped her head off**. The End. OK, sorry, that was kind of harsh. Here, have a hug. Love you, Mom!"*

The Club Foot

1642   Oil paint on canvas

Jusepe de Ribera was a Spanish painter who worked during a time of expressive art known as the Baroque period. He became well known for his dramatic but realistic works.

Hey, what did you call me?

"The Club Foot?" **Rude, much**?! How would Ribera like it if I called him "The Massive Moustache," or "The Wrinkly Prune Face?" It's not that there's anything wrong with having a club foot—or talipes, as I think you call it now. It's basically just a part of your leg (the Achilles tendon, if you're interested) being shorter than usual. But someone calling you a body part instead of using your actual name is too much!

I guess old Ribera thought he was doing me a favor just putting me in a painting at all. Posing for fancy paintings wasn't supposed to be for the likes of me. Most people were used to seeing kings and queens and all their rich pals in big golden frames. Not a homeless kid with a disability, who's **got the nerve** to not even look tragic.

I'm not going to lie, my life was TOUGH. I was on my own, on the street, begging for enough money to buy food. That note in my hand? It says, "Give me alms [money or food], for the love of God." So, yeah, some days it was hard to keep this smile on my face.

But when I was being painted, I was **feeling good**! Don't get me wrong, it's super boring, you have to stand still FOREVER. But it's not something you get to do every day, eh? And now I'm hanging in a palace, in a better portrait than most of the ones those rich dudes PAID to be in. Haha, suckers!

The V.I.P. (Very Important Pose)

So do you know what my **favorite thing** is about my painting? The blue sky? Nah, I'm from Naples. The weather's usually pretty nice there.

My big stick? Haha, that's my crutch that I use to get around. But can you see how I've slung it over my shoulder so it looks like a rifle? Ha! I'm making fun of the "military elite" (fancy soldier men) who supposedly run things. Posers . . .

Nah, here's my favorite thing. See how you can see me from head to toe, and kind of like you're looking up at me? Well, traditionally only **kings** and other important and powerful people were painted full-length like this. I like to think Ribera saw something special in little old me, too!

MUHAMMAD SARIF & MUHAMMAD MURAD SAMARQANDI (AROUND 17TH CENTURY)

The Reader

1600–1615   Watercolor paint and gold on paper

Muhammad Sarif and Muhammad Murad Samarqandi were artists in the early 17th century. They probably worked in Bukhara (in present-day Uzbekistan), where this work was found.

I really don't like being interrupted while I'm reading. Are you the same? I was telling Mona Lisa the other day, I never envy her because I couldn't handle the noise of the crowds she gets! Anyway, if you're a **bookworm** like me, you'll appreciate this work of art that I'm starring in . . . Because it's a page from the front of a book! Ooh, funny to think that I'm reading a book in an illustration in a book, which you're seeing in a book. Pretty brain-twisting stuff!

Did you notice how my book opens upward, not sideways? It's a special type of book, called a **safina**, from the Islamic world. (That's where I'm from—my page was found in Bukhara, in what you now call Uzbekistan.) A safina is usually for essays and poetry. The book I'm reading actually contains a poem about forgiveness. Weirdly, experts knew that without me telling them! Can you guess how?

OK, look at the blue horizontal line to the left of my arm. Can you see words in Arabic, painted in white? They're from the poem in my book! There are a couple more pieces of Arabic writing, too—a signature for each of the two artists who created my page (Sarif did everything inside my twisty golden frame, Samarqandi did everything outside it). Can you spot the signatures? Hint: one's near my butt, the other's on a blue rock! It took me a while to spot them, too.

Busy and beautiful

Hello there! Where on earth shall we start? My page is a feast for the eyes, right? **Let's play a game**—you can grab a friend or family member, if you like. Set a timer for 30 seconds and try to find as many people and animals as you can!

Then try it again with trees, flowers, leaves and rocks. And again with human-made things like vases, cups and even musical instruments. There's so much to find!

Notice how many people and animals there are in my robe alone? It's a pretty unique design—they all curl around each other to make a pattern.

The Great Sphinx of Tanis

around 2600 BCE   Pink granite

This large sphinx was found in Tanis, a site in Lower Egypt. This was a name for the part of Egypt that lies north of Cairo and is closest to the sea, where the river Nile reaches the Mediterranean. Further south lay Middle Egypt and Upper Egypt.

Who goes there?! Well, don't just gawk at me, however understandable that may be. **Explain yourself!** You must either be very brave or very foolish to awaken the Great Sphinx of Tanis. For I am both **king of beasts and king of humans**! I have the body of a lion and the head of a pharaoh (that's the supreme ruler of ancient Egypt, in case you didn't pay attention in History class).

And that's just the start of it! See, experts believe my lion body represents the sun god Ra. And the pharaoh, who gives me my head, was worshipped as a god in human form. So you could say I'm a DOUBLE god. Oooohh, I like the sound of that.

Of course, such a mighty symbol of power and mystery needs to be **suitably majestic.** And aren't I, from my face's strong, still features to my paws' long spiked claws? I'm taller than most humans, over twice the length of most lions, and I was carved from a single block of granite weighing more than 11 tons—that's as heavy as five or six average-size cars (or so I hear). How puny do you feel right now, hmm?

It should be no surprise that I, like many other sphinxes, was created to guard the entrance to an important building, probably a temple. I mean, who would dare to cross me? Although actually you still seem to be here . . . Hmm, am I losing my touch?

Pharaohs not playing fair

You know, even for ancient Egypt, I'm **ancient**. Over the centuries, pharaohs came and went, and many of them understandably took a liking to me. So what did they do?

They **carved their names** into my chest and shoulders! Can you believe it? Like I'm nothing more than a wall to be "tagged" with graffitied names, as people do now. The thing is, no one knows for sure which pharaoh I was originally supposed to be.

I have the classic pharaoh's "nemes" (striped headdress), the "uraeus" (cobra) on the forehead, and the straight, plaited ceremonial beard. But that was all part of the pharaoh "look," so it's not much help!

MULTIPLE ARCHITECTS
The Louvre

1190–present   Stone, glass, metal, and other materials

Many architects have contributed to the Louvre. Among them are Renaissance architect Pierre Lescot, 17th-century architects Jacques Lemercier and Louis Le Vau, Napoleon Bonaparte's architect, Charles Percier, and, in the 20th century, Chinese-American architect I. M. Pei.

You've met more than a few of the Louvre's most famous masterpieces, right? But can you guess how many artworks it has on show in total? I'll give you a sec . . .

It's about **35,000!** So if you saw 100 works of art a day, it would still take you almost an entire year to get through the whole collection. Wow. And you know what? I'd say it's 35,001 artworks—because it's easy to forget that the Louvre, as well as being the biggest art gallery in the world, is a pretty impressive work of art itself.

We don't always think of buildings as artworks: you might not sit and gaze at your home, or your school, or your local shopping mall. But maybe you should! Because, yes, buildings have to be practical—no one wants an artsy roof if it lets all the rain in—but an architect (a sort of artist for buildings) also decides how a place should look and feel.

For example, look at this photo of part of the Louvre. Do you think the glass pyramids were designed by the same person as the stone sections? Nope. This entrance is **really modern**, with straight lines and a simple, crisp look that shows off the shapes and the materials clearly. Can you spot the water fountains that look like panes of shining glass?

It's a whole LOOK, designed by a famous architect called I. M. Pei and built in 1989. Some people HATE it, but then again art isn't supposed to please everyone!

The oldest parts of the Louvre are more than **800 years old.** Imagine how much the world has changed since then! And the Louvre has changed with it. When it was first built, it was a castle between the River Seine and Paris's city walls, to keep out enemies. You can still see parts of the castle wall **inside** the Louvre now—and you can walk where the moats were!

As Paris grew beyond its city walls, the castle became kind of useless as a defense. So King Charles V turned it into a fancy royal palace, with the help of architect Raymond du Temple. Over the centuries, kings and queens knocked down old parts of the Louvre and had new parts built. Artists also added fine statues and other decorations to the beautiful stone walls.

That is, until the French people said "No more kings, queens or royal palaces!" and Napoleon I turned the Louvre into a **huge, public art museum**. Then, around 150 years ago, his nephew Napoleon III created the Louvre as we know it today by TRIPLING its size and joining up all its buildings around its massive courtyard. What might the Louvre look like 100 years from now?!

Ways to Think About Art

"**Hello again!** It's me, Mona Lisa. It's almost time for us to say goodbye, which I always find terribly sad. But I want to leave you with a gift. Now, I've been in the Louvre for a while, and I've picked up some great ideas from our visitors on how to get the most out of spending time with art. Try out my top ten tips and see which ones work for you! (Psst, it's fine if they don't—there's no wrong way to experience a work of art.)"

1

Give yourself time to just **LOOK** at an artwork before you read or listen to any info about it. Knowing more about art can make it come to life, but so can experiencing it without any chatter filling your head. Trust yourself.

2

Find the parts of an artwork that catch your attention and make you ask **QUESTIONS**: *Why is that there? What does it mean? Who is that? Why do they look like that?* Then try to find answers to your questions. Sometimes there won't be any clear ones, but that's half the fun!

3

Get in the habit of looking at **WHEN** and **WHERE** an artwork was made. You'll soon get an idea of what kinds of styles were popular in which times and parts of the world. This really helps make sense of things. And it'll mean you notice when something is a little different and ask, "Oooh, why?"

4

Look for the **PEOPLE**, if there are people in the artwork. Imagine talking to them. What do you think they'd be like? What makes you think that? People from other places and times may have lived differently from you, but people are still people! Try to make a connection and share a joke.

5

Look **REALLY CLOSELY** at one piece of an artwork at a time. Maybe a tree, or someone's beard, or their coat. See if you can notice the little details that the artist has used. What effect do they have? For example, darker and lighter colors can make parts of a painting look 3D.

6

Take a **BREAK**! Art can send your brain spinning round in a thrilling whirlwind of big ideas and beautiful sights, and that is TIRING. Before you wear yourself out, stop and let your brain and body rest and refuel. You'll be raring to go again before you know it!

7

Try to find two or three artworks by one artist, to get an idea of how that artist tends to make things look. Then **COMPARE** one of their artworks with a nearby work by a different artist. How do they look different—or similar? It could be anything, from the way people's eyes look to how bright the colors are.

8

If you ever feel stuck when you're looking at art, try not to worry about whether you like or understand it. Just make a **LIST**—in your head, on paper, or out loud—of everything you notice about it. Often, building up a list of simple points—"the sky is blue," "there are two birds," and so on—is one of the best ways to really get to know an artwork.

9

Rather than always focusing on the central part of an artwork, remember to look at the **BACKGROUND** and edges. Whether it's the walls and floor in a painting, or the base at the bottom of a statue, all these things are still part of the artwork—the artist chose to make them the way they did. You might even find these more interesting than the main part!

10

Try to work out how the artwork makes you **FEEL**. This can be tricky, so try on some different feelings for size. Does it make you feel happy? Sad? Peaceful? Scared? There are no wrong answers! Once you've got a couple of ideas for how you're feeling, think about what the artist might have done to make you feel this way. It could be anything, from the colors they've used to the expressions on their subjects' faces.

Timeline

around 4100–1750 BCE – Sumerian civilization

One of the earliest known civilizations! The Sumerians lived in the region of Mesopotamia, which covered parts of modern-day Iraq, Syria, Iran, Kuwait, and Turkey. They are famous for inventing the world's oldest system of writing, called cuneiform.

around 700–31 BCE – Ancient Greek civilization

Ancient Greece had three main eras. The Archaic period (around 700–480 BCE) was when city-states such as Sparta were founded. The Classical period (480–323 BCE) was famous for its art, theater and philosophy. The Hellenistic period (323–31 BCE) brought trade and migration, but ended when the Romans invaded.

711–1492 – Muslim conquest of the Iberian Peninsula

Muslim armies invaded Egypt, North Africa, and other areas of the Mediterranean in 711 CE. By 718, they had conquered the Iberian Peninsula (now Spain and Portugal). Muslim rule in this region ended in 1492, when the city of Granada was conquered by Ferdinand II of Aragon.

around 900–600 BCE – Assyrian Empire

The Assyrians of Mesopotamia conquered nearby lands and became one of the world's earliest empires. Their army was the best in the ancient world, and used equipment such as chariots, battering rams, and iron weapons.

27 BCE–476 CE – Ancient Roman Empire

According to legend, the city of Rome was founded by the brothers Romulus and Remus. The Romans built up a vast and powerful empire that lasted for hundreds of years until it was conquered by the Vandals (a Germanic tribe), who removed the last Roman emperor, Romulus Augustulus.

1190 – Louvre as castle

The Louvre started out as a castle, built by King Philippe-Auguste to defend Paris.

around 750–90 BCE – Etruscan civilization

The Etruscans lived in the region of south and central Italy. They were one of the most successful cultures in the Mediterranean until they were overtaken by the Romans.

around 3100–30 BCE – Ancient Egyptian civilization

One of the world's great civilizations, the ancient Egyptians are famous for their pyramids, pharaohs, and mummies. They remained a powerful nation from the unification of Upper Egypt and Lower Egypt in around 3100 BCE to the death of Cleopatra in 30 BCE.

around 500–1400 – The Middle Ages

This period of European history, also known as the medieval era, stretched from the fall of the Roman Empire until the beginning of the Renaissance. It was a difficult time, with many famines, plagues and wars. It was also a time when many cathedrals were built and Christianity played an important role.

1364–1380 – Louvre as palace

The castle was converted into a royal palace by King Charles V and the architect Raymond du Temple.

around 1400–1600 – The Renaissance

Renaissance is French for "rebirth." During this period in European history, there was a rebirth of interest in the arts and literature of the ancient world.

around 1575–1675 – Dutch Golden Age

During this period, the Netherlands was the richest country in Europe and was famous for its advanced science and art.

1789 – First French Revolution

This people's rebellion against the ruling classes in France began with the storming of the Bastille prison on July 14. The monarchy was overthrown and King Louis XVI and his wife Marie Antoinette were executed in 1793. Napoleon Bonaparte took over as ruler of France in 1799.

around 1980–2000 – Louvre pyramid extension

The French president François Mitterrand gave approval for the Louvre to be renovated and expanded. This included the building of the famous glass pyramid, designed by I. M. Pei.

around 1780–1830 – Neoclassical period

At this time in European history, the most popular forms of art and architecture were inspired by the so-called "classical" arts of ancient Greece and Rome. "Neo" means "new."

1830 – Second French Revolution

This was a protest against the French monarchy, who were reinstated after Napoleon I was defeated. A rebellion known as the July Revolution (July 27–29) led to the removal of King Charles X. Louis-Philippe was made the new "King of the French."

around 1600–1750 – Classical or Baroque?

Two styles dominated European art in the 17th century. Classical art, popular during the reign of Louis XIV, was strict, serious, and inspired by the ancient world. Baroque art was extravagant, expressive, and aimed to create an emotional effect.

around 1820–1840 – Romantic period

At this time in European history, many artists and writers believed the Neoclassical style was too restrictive. Instead, they wanted to express their emotions and imaginations through their art. They were also fascinated by humanity and the natural world.

1911 – Mona Lisa stolen

Leonardo da Vinci's *Mona Lisa* was stolen from the Louvre on August 21 by museum worker Vincenzo Peruggia. It was discovered in Italy in November 1913, and returned to the Louvre in January 1914.

1793 – Louvre as museum

The Louvre palace was turned into a museum and opened on August 10. Its first director, Dominique Vivant Denon, was put in charge by Napoleon I in 1802, and had the job of organizing the art collections.

around 1850–1870 – Louvre extension

The museum was extended on the orders of the emperor Napoleon III. Thousands of new artworks were acquired and new buildings were added to hold the collections.

Glossary

3D – Something with depth, height, and width—short for "three-dimensional."

alabaster – A pale-colored stone. It is soft and slightly transparent, which makes it a popular choice for carving sculptures.

attribute – A special object or animal associated with a particular god, goddess, or saint—for example, Aphrodite and her apple.

attributed to – If an artwork is "attributed to" an artist, it means experts think it is likely that the artwork was made by that particular artist, though there is no signature or other record to prove it.

background – The part of a painting that is behind the main figure or subject.

Baroque – The most popular style of art (as well as architecture and other artistic forms) in the 17th century. Baroque works were dramatic, grand, confident, and aimed to spark emotion in the viewer.

BCE – "Before Common Era," meaning before Year 1 of the calendar used in much of the world today. (Year 1 is believed to be the year that Jesus Christ was born.) So if an artwork was made in around 2000 BCE, that means it was made approximately 2,000 years before Year 1.

bronze – A mixture of copper and tin (and sometimes small amounts of other metals), often used for making sculptures.

canvas – A surface for painting on—usually a specially prepared piece of cloth that has been stretched tightly over a frame.

centerstage – A term borrowed from the theater. It refers to a subject being given a very noticeable position and therefore receiving a lot of attention.

chiaroscuro – An Italian term, translating as "light-dark." This technique uses extreme contrasts of light and shade, often giving an artwork a dramatic atmosphere.

Commedia dell'Arte – An early form of theater, originating in Italy, that featured particular characters (such as Pierrot). It was popular throughout Europe between the 16th and 18th centuries.

copyist – A person who makes copies of other people's works.

craft – A form of making, such as sewing or pottery, that generally produces an object with a function (a piece of clothing to wear, a cup to drink from, and so on). Historically, "craft" was viewed as inferior to "fine art" (painting, sculpture, etc.). The word "craft" can also mean "skill."

critic – An expert who gives opinions about a form of creative work, such as art, music, or books.

detail – An individual feature that is a small part of an artwork.

draftsman – An artist who is very skilled at creating drawings.

fake – A specially made artwork (or part of an artwork, such as an artist's signature) that is designed to trick people into thinking it is a famous work or a work by a famous artist.

fl. – From the Latin for "flourished," this means that records exist of an artist working during a particular time period, but we do not know exactly when they were born or died.

full-length – When an artist shows the whole length of a person, from head to toe. Historically, only rich and powerful people, or people who were important in society, featured in full-length works.

granite – A hard form of rock. Its hardness means that special tools are often used to carve it into sculptures or monuments.

Islamic art – Work produced by artists in Muslim societies. It often includes geometric patterns, plant and animal designs, and Arabic writing.

landscape – Natural scenery, such as mountains, fields, and forests.

marble – A very hard rock that is typically white with colored streaks and patterns. It is often used to make sculptures.

masterpiece – An outstanding work of art that is highly praised, due to the artist's exceptional skill or creativity.

mounted – Attached—if an artwork painted on canvas is mounted on wood, that means the canvas is attached (probably glued) to the wood.

Neoclassicism – Literally meaning "new classicism," this was a popular form of art (as well as architecture and other artistic forms) in around 1780–1830. Neoclassical works drew inspiration from the simplicity and balance of the so-called "classical" art of ancient Greece and Rome.

oil – A type of slow-drying paint. It consists of colored powder in an oil (usually linseed oil).

portrait – A picture or sculpture of a person, who is usually real rather than imaginary.

pose – The position in which the subject of an artwork stands, sits, or lies.

Rococo – A light, elegant, and extravagantly decorative style that was popular among artists (as well as furniture makers and other creatives) in the 18th century.

Romanticism – An artistic movement that was most popular in around 1815–1830. Romantic art encouraged the artist to express their individuality. It often focused on intense emotions and the imagination, and showed a deep interest in humanity and the natural world.

sarcophagus – A coffin, or a container for a coffin, usually carved in stone and displayed above ground. Sarcophaguses were used to bury rich and powerful people in ancient Egypt, Rome, and Greece.

scepter – An ornamental stick that rulers, such as kings and queens, sometimes carry during ceremonies (special events).

scroll – A roll of paper or parchment (animal skin) for writing on. In ancient Egypt, scrolls were often made of papyrus (pulp from plant stems).

self-portrait – A portrait that an artist makes of themselves.

setting – The place and/or time that an artwork shows.

sfumato – An Italian term, translating as "vanished like smoke." This technique focuses on blending colors gently into one another, producing soft outlines and blurry forms.

signature – The writing of an artist's name on their artwork. Sometimes artists also add other information, such as the year in which the artwork was made.

sketch – A quick drawing. Artists often make rough sketches before starting on the final version of an artwork.

statue – A three-dimensional figure of a person or an animal, usually life-size or larger. Stone, wood, and bronze are common materials used to make statues.

stela – A stone slab, usually carved with writing and decoration. Stelae were used in the ancient world to remember people or events.

still life – An artwork that depicts objects, such as vases of flowers or bowls of fruit.

studio – A room or space where an artist works.

subject – The main topic of an artwork. For example, a work could focus on a certain person, object or event.

symbol – Something that stands for something else. The national flag of France represents France itself, and the female figure of "Liberty" in Delacroix's painting *Liberty Leading the People* represents freedom.

terracotta – An Italian term, translating as "baked earth." It is clay that has been sculpted into a shape and then baked, or fired, to make it hard and strong.

title – The name an artist gives to their artwork.

watercolor – A semi-transparent type of paint. It is made up of colored pigment that the artist then mixes with water.

About the Author

Alice Harman is the author of more than 40 non-fiction books for children, including the critically acclaimed *Modern Art Explorer* (created in partnership with the Centre Pompidou). Her books have been shortlisted for the 2022 UKLA Book Awards and longlisted for the 2021 Blue Peter Book Awards. Her work has been translated into 12 languages and featured in publications including *The New York Times Book Review* and *The Wall Street Journal*.

About the Illustrator

Quentin Blake is an internationally celebrated illustrator, known for his collaborations with authors including Roald Dahl, Russell Hoban, John Yeoman, David Walliams, and Joan Aiken. A winner of the Kate Greenaway Medal and the Hans Christian Andersen Award, he received a knighthood in 2013 and was awarded France's Légion d'Honneur in 2014. In 2022, Quentin Blake was awarded the Companion of Honour for his services to illustration.

List of Artworks

Dimensions of works are given in meters/centimeters (and feet/inches), height before width before depth (unframed)

PAGE 3, PAGE 6, PAGE 8 (details)
Leonardo da Vinci
Mona Lisa, 1503–1519
Oil paint on wood (poplar), 79.4 × 53.4 cm
(31¼ × 21 in.)
© 2007 Musée du Louvre / Angèle Dequier

PAGE 10
Leonardo da Vinci
Portrait of an Unknown Woman, also called
La Belle Ferronière, around 1490–1497
Oil paint on wood (walnut), 63 × 45 cm
(24⅞ × 17⅝ in.)
© Musée du Louvre, dist. RMN – Grand Palais
/ Angèle Dequier

PAGE 12
Venus de Milo, around 150–125 BCE
Parian marble, height 2.04 m (6 ft 8 in.)
© Musée du Louvre, dist. RMN – Grand Palais
/ Anne Chauvet

PAGE 16
Rembrandt Harmensz. van Rijn
Self-Portrait at the Easel, 1660
Oil paint on canvas, 111 × 85 cm (43⅝ × 33⅜ in.)
© 2005 Musée du Louvre / Angèle Dequier

PAGE 18
Winged Human-Headed Bulls, 721–705 BCE
Gypsum alabaster, 4.2 × 4.36 × 0.97 m
(13 ft 9 in. × 14 ft 4 in. × 3 ft 2⅛ in.)
© 2016 Musée du Louvre / Raphaël Chipault &
Benjamin Soligny

PAGE 20, PAGE 21 (detail)
Georges de La Tour
The Cheat with the Ace of Diamonds,
around 1635–1638
Oil paint on canvas, 106 × 146 cm
(41¾ × 57½ in.)
© Musée du Louvre, dist. RMN – Grand Palais
/ Angèle Dequier

PAGE 22
Scepter of Charles V ("The Charlemagne
Scepter"), before 1380 (1364?)
Gold (flower at top formerly enameled gold),
silver gilt shaft, pearls, balas rubies (spinels),
blue and green glass, 60 × 7 cm (23⅝ × 2¾ in.)
Photo RMN – Grand Palais (Louvre Museum)
/ Jean-Gilles Berizzi

PAGES 24–25, PAGE 27 (detail)
Paolo Caliari, known as Veronese
The Wedding Feast at Cana, 1562–1563
Oil paint on canvas, 6.77 × 9.94 m
(22 ft 2½ in. × 32 ft 7½ in.)
© Musée du Louvre, dist. RMN – Grand Palais
/ Angèle Dequier

PAGE 28, PAGE 29 (detail)
Jean Baptiste Siméon Chardin
The Ray, 1728
Oil paint on canvas, 114.5 × 146 cm
(45 × 57½ in.)
© Musée du Louvre, dist. RMN – Grand Palais
/ Angèle Dequier

PAGE 30
Jean Auguste Dominique Ingres
The Valpinçon Bather, 1808
Oil paint on canvas, 146 × 97.5 cm
(57½ × 38⅜ in.)
© Musée du Louvre, dist. RMN – Grand Palais
/ Angèle Dequier

PAGE 32
Judith Leyster
The Carousing Couple, 1630
Oil paint on wood, 68 × 57 cm (26¾ × 22⅜ in.)
Photo RMN – Grand Palais (Louvre Museum) /
Franck Raux

PAGE 34
Stela of Nefertiabet, 2590–2533 BCE
Painted limestone, 37.7 × 52.5 × 8.3 cm
(14⅞ × 20⅝ × 3¼ in.)
© 2013 Musée du Louvre / Christian Décamps

PAGE 37
Detail of mural, around 1479–1425 BCE
Mural, 68 × 94 cm (26⅞ × 37⅛ in.)
Photo Louvre Museum, Dist. RMN-Grand
Palais / Christian Décamps

PAGE 38, PAGE 39 (detail)
Eugène Delacroix
Liberty Leading the People (July 28, 1830), 1830
Oil paint on canvas, 2.6 × 3.25 m
(8 ft 6 in. × 10 ft 8 in.)
© Musée du Louvre, dist. RMN – Grand Palais
/ Philippe Fuzeau

PAGE 40
Pierre Puget
Milo of Croton, 1672–1682
Carrara marble, 2.7 × 1.4 × 0.8 m
(8 ft 10 in. × 4 ft 7 in. × 2 ft 7½ in.)
© 2009 Musée du Louvre / Pierre Philibert

PAGE 42, PAGE 43 detail
The Seated Scribe, around 2620–2500 BCE
Limestone, Egyptian alabaster, rock
crystal, and copper, 53.7 × 44 × 35 cm
(21⅛ × 17⅜ × 13¾ in.)
© Musée du Louvre, dist. RMN – Grand Palais
/ Christian Décamps

PAGE 44
Constance Mayer
The Dream of Happiness, 1819
Oil paint on canvas, 1.32 × 1.84 m
(4 ft 4 in. × 6 ft)
Photo RMN – Grand Palais (Louvre Museum)
/ Daniel Arnaudet

PAGE 46
Guillaume Coustou
The Marly Horses, 1745
Carrara marble, 3.55 × 2.84 × 1.27 m
(11 ft 7½ in. × 9 ft 4 in. × 4 ft 2 in.)
Left: © 1997 Musée du Louvre / Pierre Philibert
Right: © 1997 Musée du Louvre / Pierre
Philibert

PAGE 48, PAGE 51 (detail)
Théodore Géricault
The Raft of the Medusa, 1818–1819
Oil paint on canvas, 4.9 × 7.16 m
(16 ft 1 in. × 23 ft 6 in.)
© Musée du Louvre, dist. RMN – Grand Palais
/ Angèle Dequier

PAGE 52
Monzon Lion, around 1100–1300
Bronze, 31.5 × 54.5 × 13.7 cm
(12⅜ × 21⅜ × 5⅜ in.)
Photo RMN – Grand Palais (Louvre Museum)
/ Hervé Lewandowski

PAGE 54
Johannes Vermeer
The Lacemaker, around 1669–1670
Oil paint on canvas mounted on wood,
24 × 21 cm (9⅜ × 8¼ in.)
© 2005 Musée du Louvre / Angèle Dequier

PAGE 58
Sarcophagus of the Spouses,
around 520–510 BCE
Painted terracotta, 1.14 × 1.9 m (3.7 ft × 6.2 ft)
© Musée du Louvre, dist. RMN – Grand Palais
/ Philippe Fuzeau

PAGE 60
Claude Lorrain
Cleopatra Disembarking at Tarsus,
around 1642–1643
Oil paint on canvas, 1.19 × 1.68 m
(3 ft 10¾ in. × 5 ft 6 in.)
Photo RMN – Grand Palais (Louvre Museum) /
Stéphane Maréchalle

PAGE 62
Giuseppe Arcimboldo
Summer, 1573
Oil paint on canvas, 76 × 64 cm (30 × 25⅛ in.)
Photo RMN – Grand Palais (Louvre Museum) /
Jean-Gilles Berizzi

PAGE 64
The Winged Victory of Samothrace,
around 190 BCE
Parian marble (statue), Gray Lartos marble
(ship and plinth); statue 2.75 m (9 ft),
ship 2 m (6 ft 7 in.), plinth 36 cm (14⅛ in.);
overall height 5.11 m (16 ft 9 in.)
© 2014 Musée du Louvre / Antoine Mongodin

PAGE 66
Jean-Antoine Watteau
Pierrot, around 1718–1719
Oil paint on canvas, 1.85 × 1.5 m
(6 ft × 4 ft 11 in.)
© Musée du Louvre, dist. RMN – Grand Palais
/ Angèle Dequier

PAGES 68–69, PAGE 70 (details)
Jacques-Louis David
The Consecration of the Emperor Napoleon (or
*The Consecration of Emperor Napoleon I and
the Coronation of Empress Josephine in Notre-
Dame Cathedral, Paris, December 2, 1804*),
1806–1807
Oil paint on canvas, 6.21 × 9.79 m
(20 ft 4½ in. × 32 ft 1½ in.)
© Musée du Louvre, dist. RMN – Grand Palais
/ Angèle Dequier

PAGE 72, PAGE 73 (detail)
Statue of Ebih-Il, around 2400 BCE
Alabaster, with shell, lapis lazuli, and bitumen,
52.5 × 20.6 × 30 cm (20⅝ × 8⅛ × 11⅞ in.)
© 2011 Musée du Louvre / Raphaël Chipault

PAGE 74
Élisabeth Vigée-Le Brun
Self-Portrait with her Daughter Julie, 1789
Oil paint on wood, 130 × 94 cm (51⅛ × 37 in.)
© Musée du Louvre, dist. RMN – Grand Palais
/ Angèle Dequier

PAGE 76
Jusepe de Ribera
The Club Foot, 1642
Oil paint on canvas, 164 × 94 cm (64½ × 37 in.)
© Musée du Louvre, dist. RMN – Grand Palais
/ Angèle Dequier

PAGE 78
**Muhammad Sarif & Muhammad Murad
Samarqandi**
The Reader, 1600–1615
Watercolor paint and gold on paper,
page 36.9 × 25 cm (14½ × 9⅞ in.),
frame 22.1 × 14.2 cm (8⅝ × 5⅝ in.),
inside frame 19.6 × 11.5 cm (7¾ × 4½ in.)
© 2007 Musée du Louvre / Claire Tabbagh
/ Collections Numériques

PAGE 80
The Great Sphinx of Tanis, around 2600 BCE
Pink granite, 1.83 × 4.8 × 1.54 m
(5 ft 11 in. × 15 ft 9 in. × 5 ft)
© Musée du Louvre, dist. RMN – Grand Palais
/ Christian Décamps

PAGE 82
The Louvre Pyramid
© Musée du Louvre, dist. RMN – Grand Palais
/ Olivier Ouadah

Index

For Willa and David—A. H.

Published in association with Musée du Louvre

Mona Lisa and the Others © 2023 Thames & Hudson Ltd, London
Text © 2023 Alice Harman
Illustrations © 2023 Quentin Blake

First published in the United States of America in 2023 by
Thames & Hudson Inc., 500 Fifth Avenue, New York, New York 10110

Library of Congress Control Number 2021952541

ISBN 978-0-500-65274-9

Printed and bound in China by C & C Offset Printing Co. Ltd